INTERNALIZING STRENGTHS

AN OVERLOOKED WAY OF OVERCOMING WEAKNESSES IN MANAGERS

INTERNALIZING STRENGTHS

AN OVERLOOKED WAY OF
OVERCOMING WEAKNESSES IN MANAGERS

Robert E. Kaplan

Center for Creative Leadership
Greensboro, North Carolina

The Center for Creative Leadership is an international, nonprofit educational institution founded in 1970 to advance the understanding, practice, and development of leadership for the benefit of society worldwide. As a part of this mission, it publishes books and reports that aim to contribute to a general process of inquiry and understanding in which ideas related to leadership are raised, exchanged, and evaluated. The ideas presented in its publications are those of the author or authors.

The Center thanks you for supporting its work through the purchase of this volume. If you have comments, suggestions, or questions about any Center publication, please contact John R. Alexander, President, at the address given below.

Center for Creative Leadership
Post Office Box 26300
Greensboro, North Carolina 27438-6300

Center for
Creative Leadership
leadership. learning. life.

©1999 Center for Creative Leadership

CCL No. 182

Library of Congress Cataloging-in-Publication Data

Kaplan, Robert E.
    Internalizing strengths : an overlooked way of overcoming weaknesses in managers / by Robert E. Kaplan.
      p. cm.
    ISBN 1-882197-49-6
    1. Executive ability—Psychological aspects. 2. Executives—Psychology. I. Title.
HD38.2.K3755 1999
658.4'09—dc21   99-29770
                                                                 CIP

Table of Contents

Preface

The thesis of this report, that looking at strengths can help managers develop, is something my colleagues and I have discovered in our work with senior managers. Over the past several years I have joined forces first with a team at the Center for Creative Leadership in Greensboro, North Carolina, and then with a team in my own consulting firm to find ways to help executives develop their capabilities and increase their effectiveness.

Our work with individual executives takes the form of an intense, longitudinal development program, which affords significant opportunities for executives to grow and for us to learn how better to help them do that. We collect large quantities of data of different types about each executive we work with. We go to a lot of trouble to figure out, systematically, what these data say about the individual. We focus hard on his or her behavior, as well as what drives this behavior. Then, in collaboration with the executive, we get to the bottom of performance deficiencies.

Following the assessment we stay involved over time, as the individual attempts to put insights into practice. An ongoing relationship enables us not only to assist each executive but to understand what is useful.

In the last three years of doing this work, we have discovered that assessment should involve more than delivering the bad news and finding ways to address it. A problem-centered intervention isn't the entire answer to a successful developmental experience. We have come to see that encouraging executives to recognize and internalize their strengths has as much to do with the success of the experience as presenting them with their deficits. This counterintuitive strategy of having managers come to grips with their strengths has proven to be extremely useful since we have explicitly and deliberately employed it.

This report documents our ideas about this technique and some of the ways we have used it.

Acknowledgments

I would like to thank the following people for reviewing an earlier draft of the paper: David DeVries, Bill Drath, Rebecca Henson, Bill Hodgetts, Rob Kaiser, Rebecca Kaplan, Denise Lyons, Connie McArthur, and Amy Webb.

Introduction

A primary responsibility of effective leaders is to develop key people as well as themselves. In the area of leadership studies, quite a bit is known about how managers develop. We know, for example, that much of it happens on the job; challenging jobs, for example, can bring out latent capability.[1]

Another common way of helping managers to develop is to confront them with their shortcomings. If job challenges pull capability out of managers, feedback (especially 360-degree feedback) is intended to strongly encourage managers to correct their weaknesses. This is an effective way to address performance issues, although, as you will see, not the only way.

The purpose of this report is to call attention to a kind of development that goes beyond addressing shortcomings, yet one that is often overlooked. I propose that much of the energy spent in developing managers is channeled into getting them to see and take seriously their deficits, but what is often not considered is that it may be equally valuable to help managers recognize and internalize their strengths. A counterintuitive notion—yes, but one that is borne out if one takes a close look at the stance that many managers take to their strengths.

The report begins with the idea that the failure to recognize one's strengths is, in fact, at the root of many performance problems. Next I take up the difficulty of getting through to managers about their strengths. Following that I treat the gains that can be realized from internalizing strengths. Finally, I identify a series of principles to guide practitioners in using strengths as leverage for helping managers develop.

Certainly recognizing strengths as developmental tools has relevance for anyone in the field of management or executive development. No less so, it has value for managers at all levels seeking to grow and improve. It is also a useful idea for supervisors at any level to keep in mind when they enter performance appraisals and coaching conversations with their direct reports.

---

[1] McCall, M. W., Jr., Lombardo, M. M., & Morrison, A. M. (1988). *The Lessons of Experience: How Successful Executives Develop on the Job.* Lexington, MA: Lexington Books.

How the Failure to Recognize Strengths
Affects Executive Performance

Not fully recognizing one's strengths, far from being a mere curiosity about managerial high achievers, is actually at the root of many performance problems. Not appreciating that they are already strong in a certain area—not knowing their own strength, as it were—managers tend to overuse it or they tend to overinvest in developing it.

This link between performance problems and managers' relation to their strengths is critical. One senior manager, understanding this connection, said about the top person in his company, "If he internalized his strengths, a lot of his weaknesses would go away. It's because he doesn't accept his strengths that these weaknesses exist." Seeing that link can help executives and their coaches alike avoid working away on the presenting symptoms while failing to get at the nonobvious root cause.

There is one attribute, more frequently than any other specific skill or trait, that our executive clients underestimate in themselves. Of all the many things that executives, the majority of them "overachieving perfectionists" (as one of their number called them), must do or be to meet the diverse, continually changing demands placed on them, what could that one thing be? Is it presentation skills, conflict management, sensitivity to people, long-range planning, leadership ability? No, it is intelligence. The tendency to underestimate one's intelligence can turn out to be responsible for an executive's performance problem.

It is striking when those individuals viewed as clearly above average intellectually see themselves as merely average compared to their cohorts, as nothing special. One exceptionally smart executive, whose trademark in his company was intellectual leadership, told us, "I always had the feeling that people around me were brighter." He went on to say, "I was fortunate to be fairly bright."

Another executive, let us call him Avery Stout, was described by fifteen or twenty of his coworkers responding to a open-ended question about his strengths as very intelligent. The fact that three-quarters of this group volunteered this characteristic completely unprompted was a statement in itself. On top of that, many used superlatives. A superior: "He's highly intelligent; very, very bright; I'm sure he has a very high IQ; I think he is a very bright lightbulb." A peer: "He is clearly very, very smart." Another peer: "First of all, he's brilliant." A third peer: "I think his greatest strength is his intelligence." A subordinate: "I think he is very intelligent, extremely intelligent."

Another subordinate: "I'd say his major strength is his intelligence." A third subordinate: "I would say his greatest strengths are that he is very bright and quick on his feet."

Although Avery himself cited "above-average intellect" as one of his strengths, he responded in the feedback session to the entire section of strengths by saying, "I am surprised at the comments about brilliance and being very, very smart. I rank myself as [only] above average."

He actually carried on a running debate with some of his subordinates and peers about how smart he was. He told us, "I don't think of myself as that smart. It's a core belief. I do have a good enough understanding most of the time, but that's not brilliance. It's personality and tricks."

How did this disparity in perceptions of a strength turn into a liability? Being unaware of the extent of his intellectual ability, Avery was not able to take into account its impact on his dealings with people. He had a habit of being impatient and critical in meetings with his management team. How did this rough treatment of his subordinates correspond with his inability to see how smart he was? His attitude was, "I'm not that smart and I get it right away, what's wrong with you?" He did not make allowances for how quick he was when judging how smart other people were.

Permit me to speculate briefly as to why a population of obviously smart people would look upon themselves as not especially strong in this respect. First, when you look into their histories, many of them had bad experiences in school or in their families that left them feeling inadequate intellectually. They didn't get good grades. They had trouble with a specific skill like computation that they equated with being smart. They were made to feel dumb by teachers or classmates or parents. They got off on the wrong foot in school. They had a learning disability that went undiagnosed for years. They didn't test well; their SAT scores weren't high. They took an IQ test once and didn't get what in their mind would be a high score. They didn't go to college or didn't finish college or went to a lesser college, and privately regard that as a stigma. They had an older sister or brother who was an outstanding student, and they never measured up to that standard.

The educational system lets people down. In addition to the obvious casualties, the dropouts or low performers who never learn the basic skills and therefore leave feeling like complete failures, there are the people who go on to be successful in life but nevertheless harbor feelings of intellectual inadequacy because of bad associations with school.

A second possible reason why it is common for executives to feel inferior intellectually is that the United States is fixated on intelligence, IQ-type intelligence in particular. And as a result, smart people worry about not being smart enough and have trouble being objective in assessing their level of ability. We have had people who graduated first in their class in college or law school or business school argue that they were not exceptionally bright because really bright people become nuclear physicists or win Nobel Prizes.

This discussion of the implications of downplaying or not recognizing a particular strength shows us that not recognizing strengths can result in executives' distorting their performance. They do this in three basic ways: They overdo what they underestimate in an effort to compensate, they underdo the thing they underestimate because they inhibit themselves, and they make up for a perceived deficit by making extra effort in other areas. Let's look at these now.

They Overdo What They Underestimate

Failing to realize that they are more than adequate in an area that is very important to them, executives therefore overdo it in that arena. Some executives, for example, put a premium on being responsible and as a result err on the side of taking too much responsibility. In meetings they do the lion's share of the problem solving and are too quick to take over when their subordinates run into problems.

Other executives don't know their own power. And not realizing how powerful they are and in fact worried about not being powerful enough, they overwhelm people. Their personal power is immediately evident. And they possess knowledge and skills that add impressively to their inherent power. Yet, if the truth were known, they are forever on the alert to the danger of losing power. Not being able to see straight about how powerful they are, ironically they undermine their effectiveness by overpowering people. And their fear of eroding their power prevents them from doing things that would make them less overpowering, less intimidating. They can't admit a mistake or acknowledge to people that they need to improve. The idea that to admit a weakness is a sign of strength is counterintuitive.

For a long time one executive we worked with did not know that he overdid the forceful side of leadership: "I don't see myself as being tough or powerful." After working his way through the extensive assessment report we gave him, he opened his eyes to how powerful he was and to the underlying assumption that drove it: "I didn't see until now how brute force was adversely affecting my relationships with my people. I probably thought the opposite: brute force, being on top of things, giving people insights, would lead them to hold me up [in high esteem], lead them to follow me. But I see now they also want me to ease up and let them in."

In another case, one executive's assiduous efforts to prepare for presentations actually undercuts his effectiveness. Not trusting himself to think on his feet, he uses numerous overhead transparencies as well as detailed notes. Tied to his props and notes, he restricts his freedom to think and to connect to the people to whom he is presenting. His overpreparation and the anxiety that spurs it make him less smart than he is. Feeling inadequate, he overprepares. Overprepared, he hampers his intellectual ability: "I have to prepare. I'm not fast on my feet so I have to know the material down pat. I work hard to make up for not being intelligent enough." It is not the lack of intelligence that is the problem. It is the *anxiety* about not being intelligent enough. If he could stop worrying so much about not being smart, he would be smarter.

In cases like these, executives come by their anxiety honestly. Early on in life they had bad experiences that burned these lessons into their consciousness.

They Underdo What They Underestimate

The flip side of the behavior discussed in the previous section is that many executives, not recognizing a strength, doubt themselves in that area and therefore shy away from managerial functions that include activities related to it. They hold back. One instance of this that we have seen repeatedly is the executive who is skilled with people but, not seeing the extent of his or her interpersonal assets, inhibits himself or herself interpersonally.

One executive was completely taken aback that others described him as attractive as a person. Not knowing that he had this going for him, he hung back in relationships, even at work. Another executive at pains to treat people well trod lightly, to the point of hampering his effectiveness. His matrixed role required him at times to push his function's initiatives hard, but wanting, as he said, "peace in the valley," he was reluctant to be aggressive.

An executive who had great relationships and was effective in many ways hurt his performance and hurt himself by failing to take sufficient control. What kept him from being more forceful? "Fear and wanting to please," he said. His manner, if you paid attention, gave away his uneasiness. His voice quavered ever so slightly, and there was a smooth niceness to his manner of speaking that seemed to suggest a nonthreatening individual. Although pleasant, his way of presenting himself lacked an edge to it. He was almost compulsively modest, almost afraid to take credit even when it was manifestly due him, as was evident in this exchange with his direct reports: "My team said, after the good year we just had, 'You should feel good about the results.' I told them, 'No, it's really you guys who do the work.' And they said, 'No, you focused us. We needed you to lead us.' " He explained to us what lay behind the stance he took. "They feel like peers to me. I used to be in awe of these guys." When we pointed out that he had once held the same job, he said, "Sometimes I forget. 'Forget' may be the wrong word. 'Underappreciate' is [the word]. It's hard to remember how far you've come."

They React to Perceived Lack of Talent by Trying Too Hard

Besides discounting a specific skill, executives may underestimate themselves in general and make up for this perceived overall deficit with extra effort. This across-the-board sense of inadequacy shows up in a tendency to underrate their overall effectiveness a point or more on a 10-point scale. Executives can be very hard on themselves.

Here are two of the ways they do it.

Through brute determination. Consider the pressures that this executive applied to himself. This is someone who saw himself as "not well educated," a "late bloomer," someone who had to "play catch-up" in his career. Throughout his working life and especially when he took on a new assignment, he worried, "Am I smart enough?" His response to his perceived deficiencies? "I've succeeded not by academic success or analytical ability or a high IQ. I've done it almost entirely by brute force. I take all that energy and plow it into my job. . . . Do I feel in the back of my mind that it's more brute force than talent? Yes, I think so."

Where did he get the idea that he wasn't smart? In school. "I don't consider myself intelligent: in school I had to work hard and I took it personally." Feeling that he could not count on his brainpower, he compensated by stepping up his horsepower: "I've always had doubt about my ability to lead them [my people]. I'm not that smart so I have to work hard." He has placed his faith in all-out effort: "I rely on brute force because I'm comfortable with it. I know it works."

He concluded as a child that he had to work harder than his fellow students. "I always had a lot of anxiety about test taking. I always asked myself, did I study hard enough, am I prepared enough?" His credo: "Leave nothing to chance."

What he regarded as his winning formula he had adopted back in high school. Starting in grade school, he had been only an average student. (It turned out, on further questioning, that he had never truly applied himself but did not make allowances for that, continuing to the present day to think of himself as so-so intellectually.) Why did he not study hard? Perhaps because his two older sisters were star students. He discovered he could distinguish himself on the football field. In accounting for his success, he used the same refrain: "I became a star not because I was talented. I did it through brute force."

Because this was the first time that he had succeeded out in the world, his football experience made a strong impression on him. An offensive lineman, he regularly played opposite bigger players and prided himself in getting the better of his opponent, opening up holes for the running backs or protecting the quarterback on passing plays. In the process of overexerting himself he injured his knee and had to drop off his college football team after his sophomore year.

He worked virtually all the time. He worked evenings; he worked weekends. He almost could not *not* work, for fear of departing from his anxious ideal of conscientiousness. When the possibility of easing up was raised, he worried, "If I let up, will I be as effective?" He had come to resent his regimen, yet he was seemingly helpless to change it.

In his career he has relied upon intense involvement to ensure the right outcome, to keep the organization on course: "Just to succeed I had to be very controlled, focused, planned. It was my way of making up for deficiencies."

Through trying too hard to prove themselves. Underestimating themselves in general, some executives fall all over themselves in an effort to show that they add value. It can be startling to find out that an obviously effective senior manager in good standing harbors a private fear that he or she has done it all with smoke and mirrors and that any day his or her career will turn out to be a fairy tale with an unhappy ending. A senior manager, a very capable leader in many respects, with a solid track record in his current assignment, let us in on his private experience: "It's that feeling of occasionally saying to yourself, 'I've parlayed a little ballsiness and a lot of good luck with some pretty poor competition into a position of power and money well beyond my abilities, and I'm going to be proven a complete jerk at any moment.' I feel everything's built on sand. Like I can do computer art but it's clip art."

Another senior manager told us he did not truly believe his success. The way he put it: "I'm not sure this is real. I ask myself, 'Am I really good or not? Is this really a sham?'" In response I said, "So you worry that if you pinch yourself, you will go back to being a frog." He agreed: "Yes, that's what I see when I look in the mirror. It's all kind of unreal or surreal."

This was an individual from humble origins who had made a success of himself. There was no magic wand, no princess whose kiss transformed the frog instantly into a prince. He had turned *himself*, over time, into a corporate prince but could hardly believe his eyes. He had grown up in a small town in the middle of nowhere, and no one in his extended family had ever gone to college. His sister explained the attitude he took toward himself: "I shouldn't be this good because I came from Leadville. So if I work hard, I'll be fine. He'll always say, never forget where you came from. But that's limiting."

Several months later he raised the same theme. "I'm afraid that someone like [my boss and the CEO] is going to feel I'm not as good as I am. I'm afraid if they really knew me they would see I'm an imposter. That's why I keep them at a distance and only let them measure me by my accomplishments, so I'm not found out." (We were the ones who had introduced the term imposter to him.) It is not uncommon for perfectly capable executives performing ably in their present jobs to harbor the private worry that they are in danger of being fired.

What are the spillovers on the weaknesses side of this general sense of inadequacy? Any of a number of things. Arrogance is one. Arrogant executives can come across as genuinely bullish on themselves and their ability but that would be a misreading. Behind the superior attitude, the sense that they have all the answers, lies a painful lack of confidence. They go out of their way to prove what they themselves do not believe.

Another common problem that arises from an effort to counter the feeling of unworthiness is being overly dependent on external reinforcement. These executives are excessively concerned with what other people think of them. They care too much about status and advancement and compensation and other outward signs of worth. One other often seen distortion in an executive's managerial behavior is the huge and ceaseless effort to prove oneself; that is, prove oneself in ways that don't help the cause but get in the way. It manifests itself in trivial but annoying personal habits like talking for the sake of talking.

One especially self-honest executive admitted to us, "If one of my people asks a question, I'll immediately give them the answer. Out of a need to prove myself. Rather than turn the question back to them to get them to think about it. When I answer the question, it's selfish. I'm meeting my need to be productive."

Perfectionism is a major reason why managers underestimate themselves. This is perfectionism not in the particular sense of being overly exacting or detail-oriented but in the general sense of setting unrealistically high standards or expectations for oneself and therefore, necessarily, always finding oneself wanting.

The ceaseless effort expended by high-achieving perfectionists can be understood as a faulty control mechanism, the cybernetic system by which a person regulates how much energy is expended to reach a desired state.[2] Because perfectionists set impossibly high standards for what constitutes good performance or sufficient preparation, they read each situation as requiring more work than is objectively true. They are prone to perpetually see a gap between what they actually do and what they are required to do, and they are fated to work endlessly to close that gap. Their control system registers a false reading, like a thermostat that reads the temperature of a room as being cooler than it actually is and as a result the furnace runs more than necessary and overheats the room. The perfectionist constantly attempts to improve his or her performance to meet an unrealistically high standard.

Why Talking to Executives About Their Strengths Can Be Difficult

We all know that managers can have trouble accepting the bad news about their leadership, but you might think that they would welcome the good news. In fact, it can be just as difficult for them to take in the good things about themselves. Sometimes people can't get it through their heads that they have certain weaknesses. Surprisingly, the same can be true for strengths.

Everyone is familiar with the host of ways that people can explain away criticism. They can also be ingenious in rationalizing why they should not take affirmation seriously. I've heard things like:

The business is in trouble, and I'm focused on that.

I'm in too much pain because my boss is on my case [reminding himself of his strengths might be just the tonic he needed].

Weaknesses are always tied to strengths so let's look at the weaknesses first.

---

[2] Frost, R. O., & Marten, P. A. (1990). Perfectionism and evaluative threat. *Cognitive Therapy and Research, 14*(6), 559-572.

I'm not that smart and the fact that I stand out is a function of the low level of talent in this company. I'm the queen of the sty.

People at the extremes in how they view me will converge toward the middle of the range [meaning the strong affirmation will be weaker the next time these people are interviewed].

I almost took it as an insult [when my boss said I was the smartest person on his staff]. When people say "he's real smart," they are implying that I'm not practical.

Some managers presented with a favorable view of themselves fight it outright. Avery Stout, described earlier, who was widely seen as very smart, would have none of it. When I told him what his colleagues had said about him regarding his strengths, I asked, "What is your reaction to these statements about being very bright?" Which incidentally, in Avery's case, was the first thing out of people's mouths when they responded. He shot back: "I say baloney! A lot of people on this list [of people interviewed] are a lot smarter than I am. I'd attribute these statements of brilliance to high energy and being lucky, which doesn't hurt. But I think it's hard work, and high energy is being mistaken for brilliance." He knew what he thought of his intellectual ability, and he was not about to modify that evaluation.

Apart from actively resisting, many managers are not inclined to pay much attention to information about their strengths. In feedback sessions they tend to skip over the good news and focus on the problem areas. My colleagues and I cover strengths first, and as soon as we reach the end of that section, managers are immediately ready to turn the page to the weaknesses section. They are impatient to move to the things they feel they can do something about. It is the managerial attitude. One executive explained, "I'm more energized by the weaknesses because I'm anxious to improve." He also said, in a later session as we turned to the summary of his leadership weaknesses, "This is where the gold is." Another executive, who had to be gently restrained from immediately moving on, protested his innocence. He was, he claimed, interested in the positive feedback. His wife, a full participant in the session, gently countered, "Then why did you underline the heading to the weaknesses section and not the heading to the strengths section?"

Why do executives resist the good news about themselves? For a number of reasons. They may be uncomfortable with praise, as many of us are. They may worry about becoming arrogant. They may be afraid of getting complacent. They may be afraid they won't be able to keep up the good work. We'll look at these now.

They Are Uncomfortable with Praise

In truth, many executives' eagerness to move to the weaknesses may stem not just from the attraction posed by an opportunity to improve but also from a certain discomfort with good news. It is not uncommon for people in general, not just executives, to be uncomfortable when they receive praise. They deflect it, make a self-deprecating comment, change the subject, squirm, or otherwise plainly display their discomfort.

One executive set aside a portion of his regular meeting with his team to go over his development plan. He passed around the one-page document and asked for reactions. The plan, which laid out the several changes he planned to make, was notable for the lack of any mention of his strengths. When we pointed this out, his direct reports spent a few minutes telling him what they valued about his leadership. It was a spontaneous heartfelt expression of appreciation. Choked up, he was unable to speak. He later told us he was taken aback by how emotional he became.

Why the emotion? Praise may hit a nerve. It may also touch a tender spot, the painful-to-the-touch underlying sense of inadequacy. Thus one reason that managers, who otherwise very much want recognition, dance away from it when it is offered to them face-to-face is that their sense of self-worth is a sore point. Praise simultaneously gratifies an aching need and also inevitably gets uncomfortably close to the pain associated with the feeling of inadequacy.

They Are Averse to Arrogance

With one executive, we encountered an interesting variation of the fear of praise. The assessment report showed clearly that he underestimated himself. Where his coworkers rated his effectiveness 8.25 on a 10-point scale, he rated himself a 7, more than a full point lower. Also, on one 360-degree instrument he indicated a definite need for improvement on fourteen (of ninety-eight) items on which his coworkers indicated a strength. On a second 360-degree instrument, he scored himself on six items quite a bit worse than other people did.

In the feedback session, after establishing these disparities, he and I had the following exchange.

R.E.K.: I suggest you write down in one place all of the positive feedback you've received, both the ratings and the verbal comments. Imagine you internalized that high praise. Bathed yourself in it.

Executive: See, I have trouble doing that.

R.E.K.: Why?

Executive: People would view me as egotistical. I don't like people who are like that. Also, I worry that if I got to that point [of accepting these strengths], I might fail. So fear of failure.

R.E.K.: Have you known this was an issue, that you don't recognize your strengths?

Executive: No. [Then, warming to the idea of a stronger sense of his strengths, getting into the hypothetical situation:] If I did this [felt better about myself], I think I'd be able to do better on these other things. If I do this, will these weaknesses go away?

R.E.K.: Money back guaranteed!

This manager was reluctant to take in the evidence of his strengths for fear that he would get a swelled head. He equated confidence with arrogance, a strong ego with a big ego. This anxiety-ridden confusion held him back. Underestimating himself, he shied away from asserting himself in several respects.

They Have a Fear of Complacency

Behind executives' uneasiness about praise may lie a concern about complacency. If such executives allowed themselves to think more highly of themselves, they might become self-satisfied and stop working as hard. Avery told us, "I don't want to adjust my view of my intelligence. I think that would be bad. The reason why is I think I play in an area with truly brilliant people, and if I viewed myself as equivalent, I might think I don't have to work as hard. I might relax." This attitude was actually a lifelong coping mechanism, as he explained. "Throughout my life a tool I've used is the idea that I'm handicapped. I always consider myself as at the lower end of the group I'm working with."

Avery may have had multiple reasons for adopting this stance. He was young for his grade in school. His family moved a lot. He didn't start getting good grades until high school. ("I think I may have been traumatized in school because I wasn't a good student.") A great debater, Avery clinched the argument by saying, "Why wouldn't I devalue what I have and value more what I don't have?"

Executives like Avery believe that the feeling of inadequacy has worked for them. They have convinced themselves that it is integral to what success they have enjoyed and for that reason they can be reluctant to change it.

They Feel Pressure to Keep Up the Good Work

Another of the various reasons why executives resist affirmation of their ability and performance is that they instantly feel the pressure to keep it up. A young, extremely effective manager with great potential confided in us that the reason he had trouble taking satisfaction in all the good things people said about him was that he worried whether he could continue to perform. A CEO who had just taken the helm held an off-site meeting with the two people who would report to him, individuals who had also been in competition for the top job. After a long series of discussions about business issues and personal issues, the two sector presidents told the CEO, in what was in its own way a sacred moment, that they were ready wholeheartedly to sign up on his team. The CEO said nothing. He did not seem to respond in any way, and the conversation moved on.

When one of us asked him a little later for a response to that highly significant moment, he said, "It felt great; fantastic. But I immediately felt the pressure of their expectations." Later on, he told us privately of the "terror" of meeting expectations. As a child he had been burdened by his parents' sky-high expectations ("You can be president of the United States"), and now as an adult he overburdened himself.

Another executive experienced positive reinforcement as pressure to raise the level still higher. Projecting how he expected to react to the data on his strengths in the upcoming feedback session, he said, "With mixed feelings. You want it but you get it and say, 'They're exaggerating,' and 'They don't really mean it.' And, 'Uh-oh, now I have to do better than that if they're mentioning it. Now it's out in the open and not in some secret Swiss bank account.' So with praise it's like, 'Wow, the only way I will get more praise from here on is to do better.' "

Saddled with a perfectionism that never allows them to be satisfied with themselves, managers resist positive feedback for the same reasons that they have labored for years with a discounted view of themselves. They formed that self-view early in their lives, and as painful as it may be, it has proved extremely durable, even in the face of contradictory evidence.

What Can Be Gained from Internalizing One's Strengths

There are two interrelated ways to bring one's view of oneself in line with the more favorable view held by others. Both accrue significant gains for those willing to add them to their behavioral profile. First, temper strengths that have been overplayed. And second, build up skills that have been under-played. It is a matter of having executives stop worrying so much about the things that they are already good at and transfer the excess emotional energy to where it is needed, from the strong side to the weak side.

Strengths Are Tempered

What are taken to be weaknesses are many times the effects of overdo-ing strengths. In these cases, if the managers could learn to recognize the extent of their capability, they would be less liable to take the strength to a counterproductive extreme.

Executives (as well as people in general) invest certain attributes with huge significance, operating on the assumption that this capability will protect them or will ensure their success in the world. It becomes an obsession with them. And loading this attribute with so much emotion, they cannot be objective about it. Given how critical it is to them, they never feel they have enough of it. Their perfectionism makes them poor judges in this respect. So they overdo it, and what would otherwise be a wonderful unalloyed strength becomes a weakness.

Those qualities or strategies that executives overdo are things on which they place tremendous value—hard work, preparation, control, intelligence. It is almost as if executives invest these properties with quasi-magical power, the power to save their lives in some sense. Their extremely strong attach-ment to these things is closely associated with their overuse of them.

Thus, when they come to see how strong in actuality they are in these respects, they are able to recalibrate their reading of how much is enough. This is another way in which accepting one's strengths can alleviate perfor-mance problems. When managers can learn to see what those around them see, to see how well endowed they are, they can be reassured. They can allay their anxiety that they don't do enough and consequently stop doing too much.

One executive that I worked with was talking one day about taking the pressure off, relaxing, "not being so pent up . . . about things." He hastened to add, however, that he didn't mean a swing to the opposite extreme: "By relax I don't mean become complacent or lackadaisical." At another point in our work with him he put the recalibration this way: "One way to be successful now and in future jobs is to be a little more comfortable with my abilities. That doesn't say you don't have to work hard." He understood that it is a matter of degree: "This process has helped me understand that I don't have to be quite as driven."

Two benefits that accrue to managers who take in the reality of their strengths are: they use their strengths more selectively and they make allowances for their strengths.

Using strengths more selectively. When executives begin to take in how powerful or intelligent or otherwise well endowed they are, it improves their performance by making it possible for them to use their strengths more selectively. The fault had lain in using a characteristic (old faithful) when it was not useful or using it to excess. To choose more wisely when to use a strength or how much of it to use can represent a distinct improvement in managerial practice.

Selectivity is a key word. A large part of development is learning to use one's strengths more selectively. As one high-powered and at times overpowering executive discovered, "I don't have to give up my fastball; I just don't have to throw it all the time."

When executives can strip away the excess, they are left with the effective core.

Making allowances for one's strengths. Executives may not have a perspective on their strengths or on the particular ones that have great significance for them. Because they so badly want to be good in a certain respect and because they worry so much that they are not, they have trouble being objective about that attribute in themselves. Their emotions surrounding that attribute cloud their judgment. Not realizing fully how good they are, they do not take that into account in working with other people.

When Avery read the summary of coworkers' comments on his strengths, especially all the appreciation for how smart he was, it had an impact. As a result he began to make allowances for his superior intellectual ability. His recognition helped him be more patient with people who didn't "get it right away," where before he had been rough on them.

Abrasive executives can have a difficult time putting a stop to their destructive behavior. Pointing it out to them is no guarantee that they will change, even if they resolve to do better. Immediately after the session in which one executive had his revelation about his strengths, however, his offensive behavior stopped. It was as if that way of relating to people simply dropped out of his behavioral vocabulary. Having incorporated the change in attitude, he was able to sustain the change.

A year later he did revert in a staff meeting set up to deal with a difficult business situation, but by the next meeting he had righted himself. As clear-cut an improvement as this change represented, it hardly made him a blemish-free leader. But it did remove a serious objection to his leadership as well as an impediment to his effectiveness. And the improvement stemmed from a newfound appreciation of his intellectual capacity, a view he had resisted for years.

Another executive prone to overdoing it who was ultimately able to let the full extent of his strengths sink in reported soon after the feedback session that one of the headlines was, "You don't have to always prove you know everything. People accept that you're smart and knowledgeable. People accept you're the leader. You don't have to prove it every day. They know you're the boss." One of the benefits of recognizing a strength is that you have an easier time understanding other people's reactions to you. By gaining a more realistic idea of how powerful you are, for example, you can tune in more readily to signals that a subordinate is intimidated. It is a form of taking responsibility for one's behavior.

Energy Is Freed Up for the Weaker Side

For every managerial characteristic that is overdone, there is usually an opposing, complementary characteristic that is underdone. Managers who take *forceful* leadership to an extreme often give short shrift to *enabling* leadership. And conversely, those managers who overdo enabling leadership tend to underdo forceful leadership.[3]

If managers can reduce their investment on one side of a duality, then they free up emotional energy for the other side. The side previously emphasized no longer draws a disproportionate share of energy, and the surplus becomes available for the side previously valued less. If you come to believe

---

[3] Kaplan, R. E. (1996). *Forceful Leadership and Enabling Leadership: You Can Do Both.* Greensboro, NC: Center for Creative Leadership.

that you are actually very good at something that you badly want to be good at, then you can relax on that point. You free up energy, including emotional energy, for other things.

Perhaps the best way to show this is to tell you some stories that relate actual experiences with executives.

An overly forceful type who freed himself to be more people oriented. Several years ago we worked with an executive whose reactions to his assessment data helped me see the dynamic of freeing up energy for the other side clearly for the first time. Like many others, he prized intelligence above all other traits:

> There's nothing that I'd rather have people say about me. It's probably too important.

This executive made this statement in the feedback session after he read the glowing comments about his intellectual ability. And it was insightful of him to sense that he was probably overly invested in this part of himself.

Though he had not thought of himself this way he did not resist the different view. He was able to take satisfaction in his coworkers' highly favorable opinion of him:

> I was surprised that those strengths [intelligent, analytical] were universally seen. I was insecure about them. These are things that I admire in others.

He was pleasantly surprised to learn that the very set of things that he admired in others, other people admired in him.

In caring so much about being smart he had unwittingly allowed other management functions to suffer, especially relationships. It was not just that he lacked skill, which he obviously did. It was that he placed relatively little value on relationships, and the interpersonal returns were commensurate with the limited investment. Now that he saw that he had become the highly intelligent person he had dreamed of but worried he would never be, he saw right away that he could pull back on that investment a little and invest the newly available resources elsewhere:

> What this says to me is that I don't need to try so hard to do this [be intelligent, analytical], because it's the image I *wanted* to have.

As soon as he saw that he now possessed the thing that he had long sought, he immediately drew the implication that he could expend less effort. He no longer had to prove himself in this way. It was this individual's realization that helped me to see the connection between accepting one's strengths and releasing energy to make up deficits.

In overrelying on his own intellect and underrelying on the contributions of others, this executive had come close to polarizing on the forceful-enabling continuum. He identified powerfully with the forceful pole, with being an intellectual force. And he identified weakly with and had relatively little use for the enabling pole, that is, drawing on the resources of others. When he came to appreciate how capable intellectually he truly was, he no longer needed to hold on so tightly to the forceful pole, and he immediately could imagine a stronger attachment to the enabling pole. It had been his habit to rely on his own thinking, his own thought process, and he saw now the opportunity to relate to other people in such a way that he would make better use of their thinking. With this new perspective he could now see the need to break several bad habits.

One, he had had a tendency to come to project meetings declaring, "I've got the answer!" Two, his decisiveness and his bias for action, good things generally, meant that he frequently cut off discussion and therefore did not get all the relevant input. Three, his abrasiveness discouraged some people from speaking up. And, four, in his effort to articulate his thoughts, he not only did not listen well, he neglected to draw people out.

An enabling-oriented executive who freed himself to be more of a force. From working with Jim Merriam (not his real name), I learned that even managers who got great grades in their assessment reports can benefit from taking better account of their capabilities. It would be natural to assume that this class of manager, fairly rare in my experience, would have little or nothing to gain from a feedback report that was highly favorable. It would be like going to your doctor for a physical and getting a clean bill of health. Driving away from the doctor's office, you would feel grateful that there was nothing wrong and that you could get on with your life. But your life wouldn't change.

Given the limits of what we knew a few years ago about how to use positive feedback, we made the tacit assumption that the stronger an executive's report, the weaker our position, the less we had to offer. What we learned from working with Jim Merriam was how wrong that assumption was.

No senior manager is so good that he or she can't get better. All humans, no matter how much they have realized their potential, possess significant, serious potential to improve—if they can only discover it. Jim, in fact, made a significant change: he became a stronger leader.

We knew enough to point out how favorable the data were, but we were not prepared for Jim's reaction on the second day of the usual two-day feedback session. (To protect this individual's privacy I have altered some of the details of his circumstances, but I have left untouched the words he used to describe his experience.)

The first thing out of his mouth was, "The realization was very liberating." It took him no time to start drawing the implications: "Out of this is the reinforcement that it's okay to take off a little of the pressure. Which will make other things possible. This experience has helped me recognize that there's a degree of relaxing that goes with this, which helps me in other areas." This experience of being released by affirmation we have since seen in other executives.

In a conversation three months later it was evident that the effect had held up. Jim continued to use the same language to describe it: "This has been a very nice liberating experience. It takes some of the pressure off." Intuitively understanding the importance of taking in the good things about himself, he had reread the report more than once. The realization had not faded, as it sometimes does in our work with executives. In Jim's case there was no doubt: "I have been able to accept it. It's stayed with me." If anything, the impact had intensified. He now talked more broadly about confidence and self-esteem. "This process has given me the confidence that if I get into a situation that doesn't go well, I'd still have value. I'd still be okay. That's taken the pressure off, a lot of pressure."

In a long, reflective conversation we had with Jim two and one-half years after the feedback session, he returned to the same theme. He began his account by commenting,

> There was always this feeling within me that I didn't quite measure up. I was always putting a lot of pressure on myself even though there were outward signs I was very successful—accomplishments, promotions.

The assessment report, along with our interpretation of the report, revealed to him that he did in fact measure up:

> I guess the one word that occurred to me in thinking about our conversation today is relax. It [the insight] really allowed me to relax into who I was with a degree of self-assurance. By relax I don't mean [become] complacent or lackadaisical. It releases you so you're not so pent up and you're not so tenuous.

His sense of self-worth had been somewhat tenuous. Now he had gotten a better grip on it: "You aren't always walking on that tightrope, feeling if you make a misstep you fall off that track."

If the realization was liberating, what did it free him to do? The most important thing is it helped him to become a still stronger leader.

He freed himself to become more of a factor in top management, to speak up more and to be more assertive. Jim had always distinguished himself by running his piece of the business exceedingly well, but in forums with his superiors and his peers he had taken a low profile. "My natural inclination with a group of senior people would be to be cautious, but I have stepped out more," he reported nine months after the intervention. "Previously I haven't enjoyed being thrown in with other senior people, especially superiors. This is tangling with people. I'm not sure I could have been as effective with my former point of view." Two and a half years out he continued to enjoy a more influential role in senior management. This is the change in behavior that meant the most to him:

> The greatest thing that happened to me was that this process allowed me to move into a strategist role in the company. I realized that I had a voice that was important and could be effective in shaping the corporation's strategy and that it was important to express that and not take as cautious an approach as I might have. So it helped me be a risk-taker in unknown circumstances; it's a heckuva lot easier for me to be reserved than being an outspoken person.

> I'm more effective upstream by fifty percent because I'm much more open, confident, willing to speak my mind, willing to take a controversial position, realizing that I don't always have to win the point. So from that standpoint, it has helped me greatly.

In addition to the inherent satisfaction it provided, the greater visibility helped his chances of advancing.

With his own people too he began to communicate more freely and powerfully, a change that coworkers began to see in the months following the assessment:

> I think this release helps me to be a real person with people and a genuine person. Part of this is showing what you are passionate about and what do you stand for. These are qualities that were inside of me but they were suppressed because of this baggage I was carrying around. That is part of releasing and saying I was okay.

He understood the change as becoming more comfortable being himself. In retrospect he could see that he had played a role, put up a facade:

> If you spent a lifetime acting and suppressing, I think it takes a whole lot for you to make genuine change, and you do that through being more aware and releasing yourself to be a little more open and experiment.

> It's letting a little more of my natural self out. This is liberating. I fully admit that there's a facade. With maturity and age it's faded a little. But the data have said it's okay to let the facade go away.

Interestingly, his newfound openness also carried over to his marriage. (We sometimes involve the spouse in our process, but with Jim we did not.) He reported later that he had begun to spend more time with her and to talk more personally with her:

> I can be vulnerable with her in a personal way. Here again it comes back to me feeling okay. Before, it was part of not feeling confident— you don't want to be vulnerable. You want to be in control. That's one of the things I'm working on. I'm not there. But I can recognize it and experiment.

Never one to claim more than he deserved, he said near the end of his retrospective account, "Let me assure you that I am a work in progress. I'm not there."

One reason why managers do not succeed in their efforts to fix their performance problems is that their values get in the way. As long as they place supreme value on the capability they already possess (working hardest at it because they doubt they have enough of it), and, if the truth were known, place a relatively lower value on the weaker areas, their prospects for improvement are clouded. To develop the weaker side is therefore not simply a matter of acquiring skill; it requires that executives overcome a bias against that side. Emotions enter in.

Another emotion that may come into play is fear, a fear of the other side. In addition to being attracted to one side, executives may be repelled by the other side, creating a double whammy. Many executives are attracted to mastery, to attaining mastery to the nth degree, and at the same time they are uncomfortable with relationships. An executive whose strengths lay almost entirely in the area of mastery understood this in himself very well: "I can control these talents and push them in the right way to compensate for weaknesses. I do it by keeping the adrenaline high. I build walls around myself with them and I always keep them up. I keep reinforcing them because I know the other side, the human side, the feeling side, I'm not as good at."

This is what Sidney Blatt called *defensive avoidance*.[4] People who opt in their lives for mastery and self-assertion do so not only because they are attracted to that line of development but because they are avoiding the other line. In this case the tendency to overdo strengths is overdetermined, and the challenge of correcting the imbalance is doubly difficult.

How to Help Executives Use Strengths for Development

I will concentrate in this section on how my colleagues and I as executive coaches go about helping executives internalize their strengths. This is something, however, that executives in their supervisory capacity as well as human resources professionals can do themselves, if not at the same depth or with the same power. This is also a direction that executives can take in pursuing their own development. Most broadly, don't take the strengths for granted; also, engage the executive in reflecting deeply on his or her strengths and track record; and get personally involved and stay involved. (Executives working on their own development are well advised to involve someone they respect and trust to help them with this endeavor.)

---

[4] Blatt, S. J. (1995). The destructiveness of perfectionism. *American Psychologist, 50*(12), 1003-1020.

Principle 1: Don't Let Them Take the Strengths for Granted

This principle is of course the most fundamental: Executives must come to understand that there is great leverage available in internalizing their strengths. It is so easy to fall into the fix-the-weaknesses trap. Once they recognize a performance problem, executives, being an action-oriented breed, can't wait to get their hands on it. Although there is always merit to this approach, it will at the very least be incomplete and therefore to some degree ineffective if it doesn't get at the root of the problem. What may seem to be a straightforward skill deficit may turn out to be a product of something deeper. It is fair to say that roughly half or more of an individual's potential to grow and improve may lie with the strengths.

An executive's strengths may be as obvious as the nose on his or her face. Obvious to others, that is. But they are not necessarily obvious to the individual in question.

Gifts that are apparent to everyone else are not necessarily apparent to the person who possesses them. It is a common mistake for coaches and coworkers to assume that what they see and appreciate and feel that they can count on in an executive is what that person sees, appreciates, and feels he or she can count on. It is a careless assumption, an unthinking one, but they should be forgiven for making it when the strengths in question are not garden-variety managerial skills but dazzling talents.

This phenomenon stands the story of the emperor's new clothes on its head. It is plain as day to the crowd of people watching the procession that the emperor is naked but believes that he isn't (and wants the crowd to believe that too). In this case, the emperor (that is, the executive) seems to think he is naked when it is evident to everyone else that he is fully clothed. Or, perhaps more accurately, he thinks that he is dressed like a pauper when everyone else can plainly see that he is clothed royally. In practice it is not a matter of either-or. It is not usually that managers have no idea they possess a given strength; it is that they discount it.

It may be that people fail to realize that executives don't see their strengths as others do because the impact of those strengths, especially when they are great strengths, is so powerful. Onlookers assume, without even knowing that they make the assumption, that the executives' reality is their reality. It is as if it could almost not be otherwise. It wouldn't occur to anyone to question whether these strengths exist in the individual's mind any more than it would occur to anyone to consider whether that individual sees the same physical object, like the conference table or telephone, that others do.

It has been extremely helpful in working with managers on their development to discard my previous (tacit) assumption that I could take the data on strengths for granted—that executives were already aware of their major strengths or that if they were not already aware they could readily take in and digest the news. It is interesting to me that I made no such assumption about the data on weaknesses. What has been even more interesting is to discover the impact on the executive's behavior of underestimating his or her strengths and the benefit that accrues to him or her from internalizing them.

Jim Merriam, looking back quite a bit later on his development effort, pinpointed his reaction to the data as pivotal. He recognized that his initial reaction could have taken him the wrong way: "When I got the feedback, I overlooked all the positive stuff and I focused on where I needed to improve." He understood that this was part of a long-standing pattern, the tendency to fixate on the possibility that he did not measure up. Despite the accomplishments and his successes, "always I had to look for my weaknesses because there was probably something wrong that I wasn't aware of." He could now see the adverse effect on his performance, as generally good as it was, of failing to recognize his strengths:

> I realize now that what I was doing was disrupting my effectiveness in many ways because I couldn't accept who I was. I couldn't be comfortable with myself and at times I felt I needed to play a role rather than just be who I was.

The whole notion that his job in working with the feedback was as much to take in the strengths as it was to face up to weaknesses he described as an "awakening":

> Your pointing out that I needed to accept the strengths and accept the balance in my leadership, that really was a significant awakening to me. So I learned that recognizing your strengths is just as important as understanding your weaknesses because if you can't accept your strengths you don't recognize you have a foundation. So it was realizing that I had that foundation, rather than feeling I had to search for that foundation. So I realized that the foundation was stronger than I had thought and broader than I thought it was.

In addition to having a good foundation, it does quite a bit of good to *know* you have it.

Principle 2: Engage Them in Potent Self-reflection

There are many ways to promote self-reflection effectively without bringing in an external consultant. It can happen in the normal course of a supervisory relationship, provided the supervisor takes the time to have bona fide performance reviews with his or her direct reports. It can also be part of the organization's in-house management development activities, not to mention the informal tête-à-têtes that spring up between coworkers who have a personal connection.

In our activities as executive coaches we administer, for those individuals who elect it, a heavy dose of data, with much feedback on strengths. We administer a survey to fifteen or twenty of the executive's coworkers, and we also interview them. The sheer quantity of the data is important. So is diversity in the data set. So we include several categories of coworker superiors, peers, direct reports, and nondirect reports. We also ask the executive to fill out several personality profiles that often provide clues. In addition, we routinely gather information about the life history of each executive as well as about his or her current personal life, at least from the individual's point of view. The quantity of data and the variety in the types of data combine to create a good opportunity to have an impact on the executive, not just an intellectual awareness. Also, when the messages coming from the different sources converge, that cross-validation lends credibility to the assessment and adds to the impact.

Jim Merriam's assessment report was very positive, so much so that I actually found myself worrying before the feedback session whether there was anything of value we could give him. It was evident from the comments that coworkers made about his overall effectiveness that he was held in very high regard.

> I believe that Jim is one of the most consummate managers/leaders in our company.

> Jim is a great leader whose potential has only begun to be tapped.

> Jim is the best leader and manager that I have worked for.

> In my opinion Jim has all the qualities of a great leader and has the potential to contribute to this corporation at a higher level. He is clearly a person capable of heading this corporation.

> I admire his abilities. He's been a role model for me.

The high opinion of him was also reflected in the ratings of his overall effectiveness as an executive. On a 10-point scale where 10 is outstanding and 5 is adequate, his average rating was 8.8. It is rare in our experience for managers to get an effectiveness rating that high.

Some executives are highly regarded overall and are recognized as having great leadership ability but are woefully lopsided, with towering strengths but also great shadows cast by those strengths. In those cases it is easy to identify areas for improvement. But Jim had no glaring weaknesses. He was strong across the board. A superior said, "I look for people who can cover the waterfront. Jim has a lot of it. There is a small minority of people who have that ability."

Jim got good grades on both sides of several classic dualities. He did well on strategic thinking and on execution; on getting things done and on relationships; on being forceful and on enabling others; on having "mental toughness" and on caring about people; on contributing personally and on bringing out the best in others. He was intelligent, insightful, and a quick study; he set priorities effectively, was well organized, managed conflict well, had high integrity, and so on. On the 360-degree instrument, he got good scores on an unusually high number of items. On seventy of the ninety-eight items, two-thirds or more of the raters indicated that he had the managerial skill in question.

How did Jim react? On his own he saw how positive the report was, and as he told us, he was "pleased, humbled." In going over the data with him, however, we emphasized the point. He asked how he compared to other executives, and we were able to say very favorably. In addition, we pointed out how balanced his leadership repertoire was. Following that discussion he said, "The positives are overwhelming to me." We collected enough data and made enough of their positive nature that they had a powerful impact.

Principle 3: Concentrate the Messages and Distill the Data

Even when the amount of data collected is modest, it is not a good idea to go immediately from feeding data back to goal setting. To get full value from the assessment, it is always useful to analyze the data carefully so that the major messages stand out. Given the large quantity of data that we in our practice collect, such analysis is mandatory. A month or so after the initial feedback session, which typically lasts a day or more, we hold a second session designed to consolidate the report into a definition of the individual's leadership much more compact and useful than that in the original report. To prepare for that session we go through an exhaustive process of analyzing the data.

It was in Avery Stout's second session several years ago, before the work with Jim, that I saw for the first time how executives could adjust upward their idea of their capability. I witnessed an executive take in the reality of his capability.

Early in this session, we handed Avery our summary of the long section of the report on his leadership. (By long I mean 125 pages. The consolidated version was half that length.) We asked him first to read the summary of his strengths, which consisted of fifteen categories, each of which was followed by all the comments people had made in the interviews that fell under that category.

When he had finished reading the material, we asked him for his reaction. He paused before he responded. Even the delay seemed significant. This was one of these exceptionally quick-witted individuals, quick to react, fast on his feet.

He looked up and, much to my surprise, said, "I'm sobered." "Sobered" was one of the last things I would have expected him to say in response to a quite wonderful array of leadership strengths. He said sobered and he acted sobered. What had happened is that the evidence documenting one of his strengths had gotten his attention. He had long believed that he was "not that smart." He had his reasons why. He had gone to high school and college with what he regarded as really smart people, and he didn't get the top scores on the SATs and on achievement tests that they did. His scores were high but not as high as theirs. At work, as I mentioned earlier, he carried on a running debate with some of his colleagues about how smart he was. They said off-the-charts smart, but he knew better. None of those exchanges had ever penetrated his strongly held belief about his mental ability.

Suddenly, reading the long list of appreciative comments coming from superiors, peers, direct reports, and nondirect reports, he tumbled to the notion that he was, in his company's population of smart people, above-average smart. He did possess exceptional intellectual ability. A concentrated dose of affirmation accomplished what the various one-on-one conversations over the years with many of the same people had not done. During the initial feedback session a colleague and I had brought up with him the disparity between his view and others' view of his intelligence, but we had gotten nowhere. But in the original report the comments on this topic were scattered, not assembled in one place for maximum effect.

What difference did this dawning awareness of his gift make? Beyond a general enhancing effect on his self-esteem, it changed his behavior in one respect, as I described earlier. He put a stop to his destructive behavior.

This summary stage of the assessment is so instrumental to the process of internalization that it is worth looking at another example of a realization. This one concerns the senior manager mentioned in a previous section who equated confidence with arrogance. During his two-day session we had given him an overnight assignment to list all of his strengths on one page. Our clients are cooperative, but they do not necessarily follow our suggestions, nor do we always expect them to. He did. The next morning he fairly burst into the room, animated and excited, and handed us a sheet of paper: "I started listing this stuff and holy cow!"

"So it began to sink in?" we said.

"Yes," was the answer. He had gotten up at 4:00 in the morning and done the assignment, and had also read an assigned article that included the point that enabling leaders like him sell themselves short and are proud of it. All of a sudden it all fell into place.

His task in that morning's session was to consult the data and decide what, if any, changes he wanted to make. He listed three, which we characterized as all amounting to "more nearly sitting in the driver's seat."

He came right back with, "and I feel I can drive that car and *not* be arrogant."

One of his goals was to "eliminate the aversion to confidence." (He had picked up on the use of the word *aversion* from the article.)

The breakthrough he made can be summed up in his statement: "I've come to believe that being confident is okay." He had broken through an emotionally loaded belief that had impeded his self-confidence. The cognitive wall crumbled when he was able to separate out arrogance from confidence.

Principle 4: Get Personally Involved

The data are major leverage in our work with executives, but they would not have the same impact if we did not also work actively with each executive. This includes helping the executive review the data and see what is significant. But our involvement is not limited to providing technical assistance. We relate to executives in a way that they can tell we are genuinely interested in them and their well-being; we are invested in their success. Beyond that, we are prepared to put all relevant issues on the table and to deal with the emotions that may get stirred up.

The same approach can be useful to executives in their supervisory capacity. Superiors who are unwilling to put the issues on a table are no help. But it takes more than making an announcement; it takes getting engaged, having some two-way communication. The superior has a role to play in engaging the executive in self-reflection, in arranging for data to be gathered, in identifying any gaps between the executive's estimate of personal strengths and the estimates of others, in dealing with any difficulty the executive has in seeing the light, and so on. This sort of personal engagement can be most unwelcome for supervisors who are otherwise able to step up to the toughest business and organizational situations. But it is one of the most useful contributions a supervisor can make.

Principle 5: Stay Involved

It sometimes happens that the executive gets the idea right away, but when that idea is about oneself and is charged with emotion, internalization is a much longer-term proposition. Even when executives have a realization during the assessment, they have work to do in finishing the process of internalization and putting it to work for them. Instant development is a fanciful notion. Jim Merriam is a good example of an executive who stayed with the process, and it helped that we continued to take an active interest, with periodic conversations over a two-and-one-half-year period. Jim had good instincts. He knew on his own to continue to reinforce his grasp of the strengths: "I have referred to the leadership feedback frequently. I use it as reinforcement that it's okay to relax. And to be comfortable with doing that. I find myself referring to the report when the pressure businesswise goes up or strategic decisions need to be made. It gives me reinforcement." Reflecting on his experience Jim volunteered, "The process has unlocked a lot of doors for me." This image is suggestive of a process playing out over time.

> I thought the experience was a great opening of a door that was inviting me to walk through. Even though it was a little scary on that side of the door, I have found that as I walked through there was a lot of life and light that I was missing out on. I would have lost a lot if I hadn't listened to the feedback and to what you said. And I wouldn't have known that.

In the striving, perfectionistic world managers and professionals inhabit, it is easy to fixate on shortcomings, one's own and others'. Isn't it refreshing to discover that a pathway to doing better is for people to dwell sufficiently on their strengths?

Leadership in Action

*A publication of the
Center for Creative Leadership and
Jossey-Bass Publishers*

Martin Wilcox, Editor

Leadership in Action is a bimonthly newsletter that aims to help practicing leaders and those who train and develop practicing leaders by providing them with insights gained in the course of CCL's educational and research activities. It also aims to provide a forum for the exchange of information and ideas between practitioners and CCL staff and associates.

The annual subscription price for *Leadership in Action* is $99.00 for individuals and $124.00 for institutions. To order, please contact Customer Service, Jossey-Bass Inc., Publishers, 350 Sansome Street, San Francisco, CA 94104-1342. Telephone: 888/378-2537 or 415/433-1767; fax: 800/605-2665. See the Jossey-Bass Web site at www.josseybass.com

CENTER FOR CREATIVE LEADERSHIP
New Releases, Best-sellers, Bibliographies, and Special Packages

NEW RELEASES

IDEAS INTO ACTION GUIDEBOOKS
Becoming a More Versatile Learner M. Dalton (1998, Stock #402) .... $6.95 *
Ongoing Feedback: How to Get It, How to Use It K. Kirkland & S. Manoogian (1998, Stock #400) .... $6.95 *
Reaching Your Development Goals C. McCauley & J. Martineau (1998, Stock #401) .... $6.95 *

The Center for Creative Leadership Handbook of Leadership Development C.D. McCauley,
R.S. Moxley, & E. Van Velsor (Eds.) (1998, Stock #201) .... $65.00 *
The Complete Inklings: Columns on Leadership and Creativity D.P. Campbell (1999, Stock #343) $30.00
**A Cross-National Comparison of Effective Leadership and Teamwork: Toward a Global
Workforce** J.B. Leslie & E. Van Velsor (1998, Stock #177) $15.00
Executive Selection: A Research Report on What Works and What Doesn't V.I. Sessa,
R. Kaiser, J.K. Taylor, & R.J. Campbell (1998, Stock #179) .... $30.00 *
Feedback to Managers (3rd Edition) J.B. Leslie & J.W. Fleenor (1998, Stock #178) .... $60.00 *
High-Performance Work Organizations: Definitions, Practices, and an Annotated Bibliography
B.L. Kirkman, K.B. Lowe, & D.P. Young (1999, Stock #342) $20.00
Internalizing Strengths: An Overlooked Way of Overcoming Weaknesses in Managers
R.E. Kaplan (1999, Stock #182) $15.00
International Success: Selecting, Developing, and Supporting Expatriate Managers M. Wilson
& M. Dalton (1998, Stock #180) .... $15.00 *
Leadership Education: A Source Book of Courses and Programs M.K. Schwartz, F.H. Freeman,
& K. Axtman (Eds.) (1998, Stock #339) .... $40.00 *
Leadership Resources: A Guide to Training and Development Tools M.K. Schwartz,
F.H. Freeman, & K. Axtman (Eds.) (1998, Stock #340) .... $40.00 *
Positive Turbulence: Developing Climates for Creativity, Innovation, and Renewal
S.S. Gryskiewicz (1999, Stock #2031) $32.95
Workforce Reductions: An Annotated Bibliography T.A. Hickok (1999, Stock #344) $20.00

BEST-SELLERS
The Adventures of Team Fantastic: A Practical Guide for Team Leaders and Members
G.L. Hallam (1996, Stock #172) $20.00
Breaking Free: A Prescription for Personal and Organizational Change D.M. Noer (1997,
Stock #271) $25.00
Breaking the Glass Ceiling: Can Women Reach the Top of America's Largest Corporations?
(Updated Edition) A.M. Morrison, R.P. White, & E. Van Velsor (1992, Stock #236A) $13.00
CEO Selection: A Street-smart Review G.P. Hollenbeck (1994, Stock #164) .... $25.00 *
**Choosing 360: A Guide to Evaluating Multi-rater Feedback Instruments for Management
Development** E. Van Velsor, J.B. Leslie, & J.W. Fleenor (1997, Stock #334) .... $15.00 *
Eighty-eight Assignments for Development in Place M.M. Lombardo & R.W. Eichinger
(1989, Stock #136) .... $15.00 *
**Enhancing 360-degree Feedback for Senior Executives: How to Maximize the Benefits and
Minimize the Risks** R.E. Kaplan & C.J. Palus (1994, Stock #160) .... $15.00 *
Evolving Leaders: A Model for Promoting Leadership Development in Programs C.J. Palus &
W.H. Drath (1995, Stock #165) .... $15.00 *
Executive Selection: A Look at What We Know and What We Need to Know D.L. DeVries
(1993, Stock #321) .... $20.00 *
Four Essential Ways that Coaching Can Help Executives R. Witherspoon & R.P. White (1997,
Stock #175) $10.00
A Glass Ceiling Survey: Benchmarking Barriers and Practices A.M. Morrison, C.T. Schreiber,
& K.F. Price (1995, Stock #161) $15.00
High Flyers: Developing the Next Generation of Leaders M.W. McCall, Jr. (1997, Stock #293) $27.95
How to Design an Effective System for Developing Managers and Executives M.A. Dalton &
G.P. Hollenbeck (1996, Stock #158) .... $15.00 *
If I'm In Charge Here, Why Is Everybody Laughing? D.P. Campbell (1984, Stock #205) .... $9.95 *

If You Don't Know Where You're Going You'll Probably End Up Somewhere Else
D.P. Campbell (1974, Stock #203) .... $9.95 *

The Lessons of Experience: How Successful Executives Develop on the Job M.W. McCall, Jr.,
M.M. Lombardo, & A.M. Morrison (1988, Stock #211) $27.50

A Look at Derailment Today: North America and Europe J.B. Leslie & E. Van Velsor (1996,
Stock #169) .... $20.00 *

Making Common Sense: Leadership as Meaning-making in a Community of Practice
W.H. Drath & C.J. Palus (1994, Stock #156) .... $15.00 *

Making Diversity Happen: Controversies and Solutions A.M. Morrison, M.N. Ruderman, &
M. Hughes-James (1993, Stock #320) $20.00

Managerial Promotion: The Dynamics for Men and Women M.N. Ruderman, P.J. Ohlott, &
K.E. Kram (1996, Stock #170) $15.00

Managing Across Cultures: A Learning Framework M.S. Wilson, M.H. Hoppe, & L.R. Sayles
(1996, Stock #173) $15.00

Maximizing the Value of 360-degree Feedback W.W. Tornow, M. London, & CCL Associates
(1998, Stock #295) .... $42.95 *

The New Leaders: Guidelines on Leadership Diversity in America A.M. Morrison (1992,
Stock #238A) $18.50

Perspectives on Dialogue: Making Talk Developmental for Individuals and Organizations
N.M. Dixon (1996, Stock #168) .... $20.00 *

Preventing Derailment: What To Do Before It's Too Late M.M. Lombardo & R.W. Eichinger
(1989, Stock #138) $25.00

The Realities of Management Promotion M.N. Ruderman & P.J. Ohlott (1994, Stock #157) .... $15.00 *

Selected Research on Work Team Diversity M.N. Ruderman, M.W. Hughes-James, &
S.E. Jackson (Eds.) (1996, Stock #326) $24.95

Should 360-degree Feedback Be Used Only for Developmental Purposes? D.W. Bracken,
M.A. Dalton, R.A. Jako, C.D. McCauley, V.A. Pollman, with Preface by G.P. Hollenbeck (1997,
Stock #335) .... $15.00 *

Take the Road to Creativity and Get Off Your Dead End D.P. Campbell (1977, Stock #204) .... $9.95 *

Twenty-two Ways to Develop Leadership in Staff Managers R.W. Eichinger & M.M. Lombardo
(1990, Stock #144) $15.00

BIBLIOGRAPHIES

Formal Mentoring Programs in Organizations: An Annotated Bibliography C.A. Douglas
(1997, Stock #332) $20.00

Management Development through Job Experiences: An Annotated Bibliography
C.D. McCauley & S. Brutus (1998, Stock #337) $20.00

Selection at the Top: An Annotated Bibliography V.I. Sessa & R.J. Campbell (1997, Stock #333) ... $20.00 *

Succession Planning: An Annotated Bibliography L.J. Eastman (1995, Stock #324) .... $20.00 *

Using 360-degree Feedback in Organizations: An Annotated Bibliography J.W. Fleenor &
J.M. Prince (1997, Stock #338) .... $15.00 *

SPECIAL PACKAGES

Executive Selection (Stock #710C; includes 157, 164, 179, 180, 321, 333) $85.00

Guidebook Package (Stock #721; includes 400, 401, 402) $14.95

HR Professional's Info Pack (Stock #717C; includes 136, 158, 169, 201, 324, 334, 340) $100.00

Leadership Education and Leadership Resources Package (Stock #722; includes 339, 340) $70.00

New Understanding of Leadership (Stock #718; includes 156, 165, 168) $40.00

Personal Growth, Taking Charge, and Enhancing Creativity (Stock #231; includes 203, 204, 205) $20.00

The 360 Collection (Stock #720C; includes 160, 178, 295, 334, 335, 338) $75.00

Discounts are available. Please write for a Resources catalog. Address your request to:
Publication, Center for Creative Leadership, P.O. Box 26300, Greensboro, NC 27438-6300,
336-286-4480, or fax to 336-282-3284. Purchase your publications from our on-line bookstore at
www.ccl.org/publications. All prices subject to change.

*Indicates publication is also part of a package.

7/99

ORDER FORM

Or e-mail your order via the Center's on-line bookstore at www.ccl.org

Name _____ Title _____

Organization _____

Mailing Address _____
(street address required for mailing)

City/State/Zip _____

Telephone _____ FAX _____
(telephone number required for UPS mailing)

Quantity	Stock No.	Title	Unit Cost	Amount

CCL's Federal ID Number is 237-07-9591.

Subtotal	
Shipping and Handling (add 6% of subtotal with a $4.00 minimum; add 40% on all international shipping)	
NC residents add 6% sales tax; CA residents add 7.75% sales tax; CO residents add 6.1% sales tax	
TOTAL	

METHOD OF PAYMENT
(ALL orders for less than $100 must be PREPAID.)

❏ Check or money order enclosed (payable to Center for Creative Leadership).

❏ Purchase Order No. _____ (Must be accompanied by this form.)

❏ Charge my order, plus shipping, to my credit card:
     ❏ American Express ❏ Discover ❏ MasterCard ❏ VISA

ACCOUNT NUMBER: _____ EXPIRATION DATE: MO. ____ YR. ____

NAME OF ISSUING BANK: _____

SIGNATURE _____

❏ Please put me on your mailing list.

Publication • Center for Creative Leadership • P.O. Box 26300
Greensboro, NC 27438-6300
336-286-4480 • FAX 336-282-3284

Client Priority Code: R

fold here

_____

_____

_____

CENTER FOR CREATIVE LEADERSHIP
PUBLICATION
P.O. Box 26300
Greensboro, NC 27438-6300